HSC
Health & Safety Commission

Safe use of power presses

Provision and Use of Work Equipment Regulations 1998 as applied to power presses

APPROVED CODE OF PRACTICE AND GUIDANCE

L112

HSE BOOKS

First published 1998

ISBN 0 7176 1627 4

Approved Code of Practice and Guidance

This Code has been approved by the Health and Safety Commission, with the consent of the Secretary of State. It gives practical advice on how to comply with the law. If you follow the advice you will be doing enough to comply with the law in respect of those specific matters on which the Code gives advice. You may use alternative methods to those set out in the Code in order to comply with the law.

However, the Code has special legal status. If you are prosecuted for breach of health and safety law, and it is proved that you did not follow the relevant provisions of the Code, you will need to show that you have complied with the law in some other way or a court will find you at fault.

The Regulations and Approved Code of Practice (ACOP) are accompanied by guidance which does not form part of the ACOP. Following the guidance is not compulsory and you are free to take other action. But if you do follow the guidance you will normally be doing enough to comply with the law. Health and safety inspectors seek to secure compliance with the law and may refer to this guidance as illustrating good practice.

Contents

Notice of Approval

By virtue of section 16(1) of the Health and Safety at Work etc Act 1974 (the 1974 Act) and with the consent of the Secretary of State for the Environment, Transport and the Regions pursuant to section 16(2) of the 1974 Act, the Health and Safety Commission has on 7 July 1998 approved the Code of Practice entitled *Safe use of power presses.*

The Code of Practice comes into effect on 5 December 1998.

The Code of Practice gives practical guidance with respect to the Provision and Use of Work Equipment Regulations 1998, and to the extent that they apply to work with power presses, the Management of Health and Safety at Work Regulations 1992 (as amended by the Management of Health and Safety at Work (Amendment) Regulations 1994 and the Health and Safety (Young Persons) Regulations 1997).

Signed

ROSEMARY BANNER
Secretary to the Health and Safety Commission

5 October 1998

Preface

This publication contains the Provision and Use of Work Equipment Regulations 1998 that are relevant to the safe use of power presses, together with an Approved Code of Practice and supporting guidance.

For convenience, the text of the Regulations is set out in italic type, with the ACOP in bold type and the accompanying guidance in normal type. A guide to the requirements of the Management of Health and Safety at Work Regulations 1992 (as amended) is set out from the main text in separate panels (see pages 3-4).

Introduction

What is this guidance for?

1 Power presses are among the most dangerous machines used in industry. Amputation or serious injury usually results from accidents caused by trapping between the tools of a power press. The varied work demands on power presses and the wear to which the guarding mechanisms are subject means that the integrity of the guarding is constantly 'under threat'. The operation of the press itself subjects key parts such as the clutch and brake to appreciable wear and damage over quite short periods of time. This publication gives advice on precautions that can be taken to ensure the safe use of power presses.

2 This publication contains Part IV of PUWER 98 relating to power presses and sets out the Approved Code of Practice and guidance which accompanies Part IV to help you comply with the Regulations. It also contains the regulations in Parts I and II of PUWER 98 which relate specifically to power presses, and ACOP and guidance on those regulations where appropriate.

Who needs to read this?

3 You need to read this booklet if you have responsibility, directly or indirectly, for power presses and their provision and use. Throughout this publication we have referred to the employer and self-employed people who have responsibility for providing power presses for use at work, or have control of the use of the equipment, as 'you'. Where the guidance is addressed to some other duty holder, for example a competent person, the text makes it clear to whom the guidance is aimed.

Other HSC/HSE information

4 Further guidance about power presses can be found in other HSE publications. There is a non-exhaustive reference section at the back of this booklet. Up-to-date information on these publications can be obtained from the HSE InfoLine which deals with public telephone requests (tel 0541 545500).

5 The Power Presses Regulations 1965 and the Power Presses (Amendment) Regulations 1972 (the Power Presses Regulations) were introduced to ensure that the risks from power presses were controlled. The Power Presses Regulations covered the assessment of the integrity of guarding mechanisms and key parts by regular and systematic thorough examination and testing of the presses and their safety devices. The 'daily' inspection of safety devices monitored their effectiveness. Supporting requirements, for the press setter to be trained, competent and appointed, ensured the safety of the setter and the provision of presses that were 'safe for use'. Part IV of PUWER 98 carries these requirements forward.

The Provision and Use of Work Equipment Regulations 1998 (PUWER 98)

6 PUWER 98 implements aspects of the Amending Directive to the Use of Work Equipment Directive. The primary objective of PUWER 98 is to ensure that no work equipment, including power presses, gives rise to risks to health and safety, regardless of the work equipment's age, condition or origin. PUWER 98 revokes the Power Presses Regulations but contains specific requirements for power presses in Part IV. However, some of the other regulations in PUWER 98 also apply to power presses and they are set out in this publication where an ACOP and guidance specific to power presses is necessary.

Introduction

7 PUWER 98 and its supporting ACOP and guidance, relating to the use of all work equipment, is published separately to this document in L22.[1] L22 does not contain the material published in this publication which relates solely to power presses.

Complying with PUWER 98

8 If you have complied with the Power Presses Regulations, which are revoked by PUWER 98, then you will need to do little, if anything, more to meet the requirements of PUWER 98 and this ACOP.

9 There are some differences between the Power Presses Regulations and how the new Regulations will apply from 5 December 1998. The main changes are described in paragraphs 10 to 14 below.

Scope

10 The Power Presses Regulations only applied to power presses in factories. The new requirements apply to all power presses used at work. This includes, for example, power presses used in educational and research establishments.

Terminology

11 The terms 'guards', 'protection device' and 'closed tools' are used in Part IV of PUWER 98. The term 'safety device' was used in the Power Presses Regulations.

Record keeping

12 Part IV of PUWER 98 requires you to keep records of thorough examinations and inspections, as did the Power Presses Regulations. However Part IV of PUWER 98 does not specify any forms or how the records should be kept. This means that records can be kept on a computer database if you wish. However Schedule 3 of PUWER 98 does specify WHAT information must be recorded for the thorough examinations of a power press.

Thorough examinations in exceptional circumstances

13 PUWER 98 (regulation 32) requires power presses, guards and protection devices to be thoroughly examined if exceptional circumstances occur which could affect them.

Thorough examinations of fixed guards

14 Periodic thorough examinations of fixed guards were not required under the Power Presses Regulations. The guards should be thoroughly examined under the requirements of regulation 32 of PUWER 98.

Consulting employees and/or safety representatives

15 Proper consultation with those who do the work is crucial in helping to raise awareness of the importance of health and safety. It can make a significant contribution to creating and maintaining a safe and healthy work place and an effective health and safety system. In turn, this can benefit the business in making it more efficient by reducing the number of accidents and the incidence of work-related ill health.

Introduction

16 Employers must consult safety representatives appointed by recognised trade unions under the Safety Representatives and Safety Committees Regulations 1977. Employees who are not covered by such representatives must be consulted, either directly, or indirectly through elected representatives of employee safety under the Health and Safety (Consultation with Employees) Regulations 1996. More information is contained in the free Health and Safety Executive leaflet *Consulting with employees on health and safety: A guide to the law.*[2]

Young people

17 Part IV of PUWER 98 does not contain any specific requirements relating to the age of people using, setting, inspecting and testing a power press. However, there is an ACOP and guidance relevant to the provision and use of power presses under regulation 13D of the Health and Safety (Young Persons) Regulations 1997 which amend the Management of Health and Safety at Work Regulations 1992.

Regulation 13D

Protection of young persons

The Management of Health and Safety at Work Regulations 1992 as amended by the Health and Safety (Young Persons) Regulations 1997

(1) Every employer shall ensure that young persons employed by him are protected at work from any risks to their health or safety which are a consequence of their lack of experience, or absence of awareness of existing or potential risks or the fact that young persons have not yet fully matured.

(2) Subject to paragraph (3), no employer shall employ a young person for work -

(a) which is beyond his physical or psychological capacity;

(b) involving harmful exposure to agents which are toxic or carcinogenic, cause heritable genetic damage or harm to the unborn child or which in any other way chronically affect human health;

(c) involving harmful exposure to radiation;

(d) involving the risk of accidents which it may reasonably be assumed cannot be recognised or avoided by young persons owing to their insufficient attention to safety or lack of experience or training; or

(e) in which there is a risk to health from-

(i) extreme cold or heat;

(ii) noise; or

(iii) vibration,

and in determining whether work will involve harm or risk for the purpose of this paragraph, regard shall be had to the results of the assessment.

(3) Nothing in paragraph (2) shall prevent the employment of a young person who is no longer a child for work -

(a) where it is necessary for his training;

(b) where the young person will be supervised by a competent person; and

(c) where any risk will be reduced to the lowest level that is reasonably practicable.

Regulation 13D

The Management of Health and Safety at Work Regulations 1992 as amended by the Health and Safety (Young Persons) Regulations 1997

ACOP

Power Presses

18 Young people are often exposed to risks to their health and safety when using work equipment as a consequence of their immaturity, lack of experience or awareness of existing or potential risks. Therefore you should not allow such people to use a power press unless they have the necessary maturity and competence which includes having successfully completed appropriate training. However, during the training they may operate a power press providing they are adequately supervised. Adequate supervision should also be provided after training if a young person is not sufficiently mature.

The Management of Health and Safety at Work Regulations 1992 as amended by the Health and Safety (Young Persons) Regulations 1997

Guidance

19 'Young person' means any person who has not yet reached the age of eighteen.

20 Competence and maturity are not simply a matter of the age of the worker. Training in itself will not ensure competence but it is part of what is necessary. The level of supervision needed will depend on how mature the worker is and whether they can work safely without putting themselves or others at risk. Even when they have been trained, young people need to be supervised to ensure that they do not act irresponsibly or take short cuts which put themselves and others at risk.

Provision and Use of Work Equipment Regulations 1998

Part II of PUWER 98

21 The ACOP to Part II of PUWER 98 covers, among other things:

(a) training of people who prepare power presses for use, or who carry out inspections (regulations 7 and 9);

(b) the identification of the power press, guards, protection devices and closed tools, plus the indication of the speed and direction of the flywheel (regulation 23).

22 These were previously covered by regulations by 4, 9 and 10 of the Power Presses Regulations.

Part IV of PUWER 98

23 The regulations in Part IV of PUWER 98 carry forward the other requirements of the Power Presses Regulations in order to maintain the safety levels that they achieved. The requirements within Part IV are:

(a) thorough examination and testing of power presses and their guards and protection devices by competent persons;

(b) inspection and testing of guards and protection devices by people who are competent;

(c) reporting on the condition of the press and its guards and protection devices and the handling and reporting of defects;

(d) notification of defects in any guard or protection device, disclosed during either the thorough examination or the inspection.

Regulation 1

PUWER 98
Regulation 1

Citation and commencement

These Regulations may be cited as the Provision and Use of Work Equipment Regulations 1998 and shall come into force on 5th December 1998.

PUWER 98

Guidance 1

When does PUWER 98 come into force?

24 PUWER 98 comes into force on 5 December 1998 and the replacement requirements for power presses will come into effect on that date.

Regulation 2

PUWER 98

Interpretation

(1) In these Regulations, unless the context otherwise requires -

"the 1974 Act" means the Health and Safety at Work etc. Act 1974;

"employer" except in regulation 3(2) and (3) includes a person to whom the requirements imposed by these Regulations apply by virtue of regulation 3(3)(a) and (b);

"essential requirements" means requirements described in regulation 10(1);

"the Executive" means the Health and Safety Executive;

"inspection" in relation to an inspection under paragraph (1) or (2) of regulation 6 -

(a) means such visual or more rigorous inspection by a competent person as is appropriate for the purpose described in the paragraph;

(b) where it is appropriate to carry out testing for the purpose, includes testing the nature and extent of which are appropriate for the purpose;

"power press" means a press or press brake for the working of metal by means of tools, or for die proving, which is power driven and which embodies a flywheel and clutch;

"thorough examination" in relation to a thorough examination under paragraph (1), (2), (3) or (4) of regulation 32 -

(a) means a thorough examination by a competent person;

(b) includes testing the nature and extent of which are appropriate for the purpose described in the paragraph;

"use" in relation to work equipment means any activity involving work equipment and includes starting, stopping, programming, setting, transporting, repairing, modifying, maintaining, servicing and cleaning;

"work equipment" means any machinery, appliance, apparatus, tool or installation for use at work (whether exclusively or not);

and related expressions shall be construed accordingly.

(2) Any reference in regulations 32 to 34 or Schedule 3 to a guard or protection device is a reference to a guard or protection device provided for the tools of a power press.

(3) Any reference in regulation 32 or 33 to a guard or protection device being on a power press shall, in the case of a guard or protection device designed to operate while adjacent to a power press, be construed as a reference to its being adjacent to it.

Regulation 2

PUWER 98

Regulation 2

(4) Any reference in these Regulations to -

(a) a numbered regulation or Schedule is a reference to the regulation or Schedule in these Regulations so numbered; and

(b) a numbered paragraph is a reference to the paragraph so numbered in the regulation in which the reference appears.

PUWER 98

Guidance 2

What Part IV applies to - Presses

25 These Regulations apply to mechanically driven presses or press brakes (called 'power press(es)' in this publication) which are power driven, have a flywheel and clutch and which are wholly or partly used to work metal. A power press clutch, in relation to a power press, is a device designed to impart the movement of the flywheel to any tool when required. These Regulations also apply during die proving.

26 Part IV of PUWER 98 does not apply to:

(a) presses which do not have a clutch mechanism, for example pneumatic and hydraulic presses;

(b) power presses when they are being used to work materials other than metal;

(c) power presses, processes and circumstances listed in Schedule 2 of PUWER 98 (see page 28).

27 These regulations do not apply when non-metals, hot metal or metal powder are being worked. But if they are used at any time to work metal (other than hot or powder) the regulations will apply in full during that time.

What Part IV applies to - Guards and protection devices

28 Part IV relating to guards and protection devices applies only to guards and protection devices provided for the tools of the power press and to 'closed tools'. Closed tools are tools designed and constructed to be inherently safe when properly installed since part of the tool acts as a fixed guard. Part IV of PUWER 98 does not apply to any other guards or protection devices which may be on the press, although these are covered by the other relevant provisions of Parts I and II of PUWER 98.

Regulation 3

Application

PUWER 98

Regulation 2

(1) These Regulations shall apply

(a) in Great Britain; and

(b) outside Great Britain as sections 1 to 59 and 80 to 82 of the 1974 Act apply by virtue of the Health and Safety at Work etc. Act 1974 (Application outside Great Britain) Order 1995[(a)] ("the 1995 Order").

(2) The requirements imposed by these Regulations on an employer in respect of work equipment shall apply to such equipment provided for use or used by an employee of his at work.

(3) The requirements imposed by these Regulations on an employer shall also apply -

(a) SI 1995/263.

(a) to a self-employed person, in respect of work equipment he uses at work;

(b) subject to paragraph (5), to a person who has control to any extent of -

(i) work equipment;

(ii) a person at work who uses or supervises or manages the use of work equipment; or

(iii) the way in which work equipment is used at work,

and to the extent of his control.

(4) Any reference in paragraph (3)(b) to a person having control is a reference to a person having control in connection with the carrying on by him of a trade, business or other undertaking (whether for profit or not).

(5) The requirements imposed by these Regulations shall not apply to a person in respect of work equipment supplied by him by way of sale, agreement for sale or hire-purchase agreement.

(6) Subject to paragraphs (7) to (10), these Regulations shall not impose any obligation in relation to a ship's work equipment (whether that equipment is used on or off the ship).

(7) Where merchant shipping requirements are applicable to a ship's work equipment, paragraph (6) shall relieve the shore employer of his obligations under these Regulations in respect of that equipment only where he has taken all reasonable steps to satisfy himself that the merchant shipping requirements are being complied with in respect of that equipment.

(8) In a case where the merchant shipping requirements are not applicable to the ship's work equipment by reason only that for the time being there is no master, crew or watchman on the ship, those requirements shall nevertheless be treated for the purpose of paragraph (7) as if they were applicable.

(9) Where the ship's work equipment is used in a specified operation paragraph (6) shall not apply to regulations 7 to 9, 11 to 13, 20 to 22 and 30 (each as applied by regulation 3).

(10) Paragraph (6) does not apply to a ship's work equipment provided for use or used in an activity (whether carried on in or outside Great Britain) specified in the 1995 Order save that it does apply to -

(a) the loading, unloading, fuelling or provisioning of the ship; or

(b) the construction, reconstruction, finishing, refitting, repair, maintenance, cleaning or breaking up of the ship.

(11) In this regulation -

"master" has the meaning assigned to it by section 313(1) of the Merchant Shipping Act 1995[(b)];

(b) 1995 c.21.

PUWER 98

"merchant shipping requirements" means the requirements of regulations 3 and 4 of the Merchant Shipping (Guarding of Machinery and Safety of Electrical Equipment) Regulations 1988[(c)] *and regulations 5 to 10 of the Merchant Shipping (Hatches and Lifting Plant) Regulations 1988*[(d)]*;*

"ship" has the meaning assigned to it by section 313(1) of the Merchant Shipping Act 1995 save that it does not include an offshore installation;

"shore employer" means an employer of persons (other than the master and crew of any ship) who are engaged in a specified operation;

"specified operation" means an operation in which the ship's work equipment is used -

(a) by persons other than the master and crew; or

(b) where persons other than the master and crew are liable to be exposed to a risk to their health or safety from its use.

(c) SI 1988/1636, amended by SI 1988/2274.
(d) SI 1988/1639, amended by SI 1988/2274.

Regulation 3

PUWER 98

Where PUWER 98 applies

29 PUWER 98 applies to all premises where the Health and Safety at Work etc Act 1974 (HSW Act) applies, ie to all 'at work' situations. PUWER 98 applies throughout Great Britain and has effect wherever work is done by the employed and the self-employed. Therefore PUWER 98 will apply to workplaces not previously covered by the Power Presses Regulations such as technical colleges and research establishments.

Who has duties under PUWER 98?

30 PUWER 98 places duties on employers, the self-employed and people who have control of work equipment. The duty on people who have control of work equipment reflects the way that work equipment is sometimes used in industry where there may not necessarily be a direct 'employment' relationship between the user and the person who controls the work equipment, for example, where it is hired. If you have duties under PUWER 98 you need to ensure the power presses, guards and protection devices you provide for use at work comply with the regulations.

31 Although only the law courts can give an authoritative interpretation of the law, in considering the application of these regulations and guidance to persons working under your direction, you should consider the points mentioned in paragraphs 32-34.

32 If you have people working under your control and direction who are self-employed for tax and/or National Insurance purposes, they are likely to be treated as employees for health and safety purposes. You may therefore need to take appropriate action to protect them. If you are in any doubt who is responsible for health and safety of a person working for you, this could be clarified and included in the terms of the contract. However, remember, you cannot pass on a legal duty that falls to you under the HSW Act by means of a contract and you will still retain duties towards others by virtue of section 3 of the HSW Act. If you intend to employ such workers on the basis that you are not responsible for their health and safety, you should seek legal advice before doing so.

Guidance 3

PUWER 98

Guidance 3

Employees

33 If you are an employee you do not have any specific duties under PUWER 98. Your duties are covered in other legislation, in particular section 7 of the HSW Act and regulation 12 of the Management of Health and Safety at Work Regulations 1992.

Trainees

34 If employees are being trained outside their normal workplace (for example at a college) the duty holder will be the person who has control of the undertaking where they are being trained while the employee is at that undertaking.

Regulation 5

Maintenance

PUWER 98

Regulation 5

(1) Every employer shall ensure that work equipment is maintained in an efficient state, in efficient working order and in good repair.

(2) Every employer shall ensure that where any machinery has a maintenance log, the log is kept up to date.

PUWER 98

Guidance 5

Application of regulation 5

35 This regulation builds on the general duty in the HSW Act which requires work equipment to be maintained so that it is safe. It does not cover the maintenance process (that is covered by the general duties of the HSW Act) or the construction of work equipment so that maintenance can be carried out without risk to health or safety (this is subject to regulations 10 and 22 of PUWER 98).

36 It is important that all parts of the power press and the guards and/or protection devices and ancillary equipment such as automatic feed systems are maintained so that their performance does not deteriorate to the extent that it puts people at risk. In regulation 5, 'efficient' relates to how the condition of the equipment might affect health and safety. It is not concerned with productivity. However, some production-related maintenance activities will also have health and safety benefits.

37 Equipment may need to be checked frequently to ensure that safety-related features are functioning correctly. A fault which affects production is normally apparent within a short time, but a fault in a safety critical system could remain undetected unless appropriate safety checks are included in maintenance activities. The frequency at which equipment needs to be checked will vary and depends on the equipment itself and the risks involved. The frequency should also take into account the intensity of use, the operating environment and the variety of operations. The manufacturer's instructions should also help you determine which items require planned maintenance. The manufacturer's instruction will help determine the nature of the maintenance, for example proper lubrication (which is particularly important for power presses), replacement and adjustment of parts and frequency of this maintenance work.

Maintenance management

38 The extent and complexity of maintenance can vary substantially from simple checks on basic equipment to integrated programmes for complex

PUWER 98

plant. In all circumstances, for maintenance to be effective, you need to target it at the parts of work equipment where failure or deterioration could lead to increased risks to health and safety. To achieve this you could use the following maintenance management techniques:

(a) planned preventive;

(b) condition based;

(c) breakdown.

39 You should select appropriate techniques through risk assessment and use them independently or in combination to address the risks involved.

40 Different maintenance management techniques have different benefits:

(a) planned preventive maintenance involves replacing parts or making necessary adjustments at pre-set intervals so that hazards do not occur as a result of the deterioration or failure of the equipment.

(b) condition-based maintenance involves monitoring the condition of safety critical parts and carrying out maintenance whenever necessary for the same purposes. When safety critical parts could fail and cause the equipment, guards or other protection devices to fail in a dangerous way, a formal system of planned preventive or condition based maintenance is likely to be necessary.

(c) breakdown maintenance, however, only needs to be carried out after failure has occurred but is appropriate only if the failure does not present an immediate risk and can be corrected before risk occurs, for example through effective fault reporting and maintenance schemes.

41 You may need to review and revise maintenance management measures in certain circumstances, for example if the power press is subject to particularly heavy use.

Maintenance log

42 Some power presses may not be owned, but hired, by the user. Both the hire company and the user should establish between themselves who will carry out safety-related maintenance, and the terms of the agreement should be set out/recorded in writing. If the hire company is some distance from the user site, it would be uneconomical for their staff to carry them out. Both parties should agree exactly what they are responsible for.

Training for maintenance workers

43 Maintenance work should only be carried out by people who are competent to do the work.

Reactive maintenance

44 Any action which you have taken following the inspections and thorough examinations required under Part IV of PUWER 98 is reactive maintenance - this is not a substitute for the planned (proactive) maintenance which you should take to comply with regulation 5 of PUWER 98.

Guidance 5

Regulation 7

Specific risks

PUWER 98

(1) Where the use of work equipment is likely to involve a specific risk to health or safety, every employer shall ensure that -

(a) the use of that work equipment is restricted to those persons given the task of using it; and

(b) repairs, modifications, maintenance or servicing of that work equipment is restricted to those persons who have been specifically designated to perform operations of that description (whether or not also authorised to perform other operations).

(2) The employer shall ensure that the persons designated for the purposes of sub-paragraph (b) of paragraph (1) have received adequate training related to any operations in respect of which they have been so designated.

Regulation 7

PUWER 98

45 You should ensure that wherever possible, risks are always controlled by (in the order given):

(a) eliminating the risks, or if that is not possible:

(b) taking 'hardware' (physical) measures to control the risks such as the provision of guards; but if the risks cannot be adequately controlled

(c) taking appropriate 'software' measures to deal with the residual (remaining) risk, such as following safe systems of work and the provision of information, instruction and training.

Repairs, modifications, etc

46 You should ensure that where the risks from the use of work equipment cannot be adequately controlled by hardware measures, such as guards and/or protection devices during repair, maintenance, or other similar work, only persons who have received sufficient information, instruction and training to enable them to carry out the work safely should do the work. They shall be the designated person for the purpose of this regulation.

Setting, etc

47 Designated persons include those who carry out setting, re-setting, adjustment or trying out the tools on a power press or who install or adjust any guard and/or protection device preparatory to production or die-proving. A person undergoing training to become a setter may carry out this work providing they are acting under the immediate supervision of a person already designated.

ACOP 7

PUWER 98

48 Before people are allowed to carry out setting duties on their own, you should check that they:

(a) have been adequately trained;

(b) are competent to carry out the duties;

(c) have been specifically designated;

for every power press, guard and protection device they will work on.

Guidance 7

PUWER 98

49 It is good practice to record that people have been designated to do this work by making entries in a register or by attaching certificates of designation to it. You can also keep a record of:

(a) people undergoing training (including specifying which designated people should supervise their work);

(b) the power presses, guards and protection devices for which the person is designated or being trained;

(c) the fact that someone is no longer designated.

Guidance 7

Copies of the appropriate records can be given to the person concerned.

PUWER 98

50 You should ensure that the training provided for the designated person includes suitable and sufficient practical instruction in the areas outlined below, for each type of power press and guards and/or protection device for which it is proposed to designate the person being trained to become a setter:

(a) power press mechanisms, particularly their safety aspects and including the nature and function of clutch mechanisms, flywheels, brakes and ancillary equipment;

(b) guards and protection devices - types and functions of each type of guard or protection device, including closed tools where used; method of installation;

(c) the causes and prevention of accidents involving power presses;

(d) the work of the tool setter - safe methods of working, lubrication and co-operation with the press operator;

ACOP 7

(e) tool design - in relation to safe systems of work.

PUWER 98
Guidance 7

51 A designated person can be trained either on an external training course and/or at the workplace. Wherever training takes place, it should include appropriate practical instruction on the topics listed.

Regulation 8

Information and instructions

PUWER 98

(1) Every employer shall ensure that all persons who use work equipment have available to them adequate health and safety information and, where appropriate, written instructions pertaining to the use of the work equipment.

(2) Every employer shall ensure that any of his employees who supervises or manages the use of work equipment has available to him adequate health and safety information and, where appropriate, written instructions pertaining to the use of the work equipment.

(3) Without prejudice to the generality of paragraphs (1) or (2), the information and instructions required by either of those paragraphs shall include information and, where appropriate, written instructions on -

(a) the conditions in which and the methods by which the work equipment may be used;

Regulation 8

PUWER 98

Regulation 8

(b) foreseeable abnormal situations and the action to be taken if such a situation were to occur; and

(c) any conclusions to be drawn from experience in using the work equipment.

(4) Information and instructions required by this regulation shall be readily comprehensible to those concerned.

PUWER 98

Guidance 8

How regulation 8 links with other health and safety law

52 This regulation builds on the general duty in the HSW Act to provide employees with the information and instructions that are necessary to ensure, so far as is reasonably practicable, their health and safety. It also links with the general requirement in the Management of Health and Safety at Work Regulations 1992 to provide information to employees relating to their health and safety. The Health and Safety (Consultation with Employees) Regulations 1996 requires employers to consult their employees on the information requires under other regulations, including PUWER 98, about risks to their health and safety and the preventative measures in place.

What does regulation 8 require?

53 Regulation 8 places a duty on employers to make available all relevant health and safety information and, where appropriate, written instructions on the use of power presses to their workforce. Workers and managers should have easy access to such information and instructions and be able to understand them.

What should be made available?

54 Regulations 8(1) and 8(2) refer to written instructions. This can include the information provided by manufacturers or suppliers of power presses, such as instruction sheets or manuals, instruction placards, warning labels and training manuals. It can also include in-house instructions and those from training courses. There are duties on manufacturers and suppliers to provide sufficient information, including drawings, to enable the correct installation, safe operation and maintenance of power presses. You should ask or check that they are provided.

Who should the information and instructions be made available to?

55 You should ensure that any written instructions are available to the people directly using power presses. You should also ensure that instructions are made available to other appropriate people; for example, that maintenance instructions are made available or passed to the people involved in maintaining your power presses.

What information do supervisors and managers require?

56 It is essential that supervisors and managers, as well as operators, have access to the information and written instructions. The amount of detailed health and safety information they will need to have immediately available for day-to-day operation of production lines will vary, but it is important that they know what information is available and where it can be found.

How the information and instructions should be made available

57 Information can be made available in writing, or verbally where it is considered sufficient. It is your responsibility to decide what is appropriate,

PUWER 98

taking into consideration the individual circumstances. Where there are complicated or unusual circumstances, the information should be in writing. Other factors need to be taken into consideration, such as the degree of skill of the workers involved, their experience and training, the degree of supervision and the complexity and length of the particular job.

58 The information and written instructions should be easy to understand. They should be in clear English and/or other languages if appropriate for the people using them. They should be set out in logical order with illustrations where appropriate. Standard symbols should be used.

59 You should give special consideration to any employees with language difficulties or with disabilities which could make it difficult for them to receive or understand the information or instructions. You may need to make special arrangements in these cases.

What the information and instructions should cover

60 Any information and written instructions you provide should cover:

(a) all health and safety aspects arising from the use of the power presses,

(b) any limitations on their use;

(c) any foreseeable difficulties that could arise; and

(d) the methods to deal with them.

Using any conclusions drawn from experience of using the power presses, you should either record these conclusions or take steps to ensure that all appropriate members of the workforce are aware of them.

Guidance 8

Regulation 9

Training

PUWER 98

(1) Every employer shall ensure that all persons who use work equipment have received adequate training for purposes of health and safety, including training in the methods which may be adopted when using the work equipment, any risks which such use may entail and precautions to be taken.

(2) Every employer shall ensure that any of his employees who supervises or manages the use of work equipment has received adequate training for purposes of health and safety, including training in the methods which may be adopted when using the work equipment, any risks which such use may entail and precautions to be taken.

Regulation 9

PUWER 98

Training appointed people

61 You should provide training for people appointed under regulation 33 (1)(a) to inspect power presses which includes suitable and sufficient practical instruction in the following areas in relation to each type of power press and guard and/or protection device used in respect of which it is proposed to appoint the person being trained:

(a) power press mechanisms, particularly their safety aspects and including the nature and function of clutch mechanisms, flywheels, brakes and ancillary equipment;

ACOP 9

PUWER 98

ACOP 9

(b) guards and protection devices - types and functions of each type of guard or protection device, including closed tools where used; method of installation;

(c) the causes and prevention of accidents involving power presses;

(d) the work of the tool setter - safe methods of working, lubrication and co-operation with the press operator;

(e) tool design - in relation to safe systems of work;

(f) how to carry out an inspection and test of the guard protection device or closed tool, including how to detect defects.

PUWER 98

Guidance 9

62 The training needed under regulation 9(1) for a person appointed to inspect guards and protection devices can be undertaken at an external course and/or in the workplace. Wherever it takes place, it should include appropriate practical instruction on the topics listed. It is not possible to give precise guidance for the content of the training as this will depend on the duties involved in each case.

When is training necessary?

63 Press operators are most likely to need training when they are recruited. However, training needs are also required:

(a) if the risks to which people are exposed change;

(b) if new equipment or technology is introduced;

(c) if the system of work changes.

Training managers and supervisors

64 Regulation 9(2) requires you to provide adequate training for people who supervise or manage the use of power presses. 'Use' of a press includes not only production, but also other activities, in particular setting by the designated person and the 'daily' inspection and test by the appointed person (see paragraphs 129-133). Such training should include the safe operation of the press and the risks posed to the person carrying out the work (for example the press operator, setter or appointed person) as well as the quality of the inspection and test carried out by the appointed person.

Refresher training

65 You should provide refresher training if necessary. Skills decline if they are not used regularly. Pay particular attention to people who deputise for others on occasions - they may need more frequent refresher training than those who do the work regularly.

When should training take place?

66 The Management of Health and Safety at Work Regulations 1992 specify that health and safety training should take place within working hours.

Regulation 23

Markings

PUWER 98
Regulation 23

Every employer shall ensure that work equipment is marked in a clearly visible manner with any marking appropriate for reasons of health and safety.

PUWER 98

67 For work equipment in general, including power presses, there are many circumstances in which marking of equipment is appropriate for health or safety reasons. For example, stop and start controls for equipment need to be identified.

68 You should consider any other marking that might be appropriate, for example numbering machines to aid identification, particularly if the controls or isolators for the machines are not directly attached to them and there could otherwise be confusion.

69 Markings may use words, letters, numbers, or symbols, and the use of colour or shape may be significant. There are nationally or internationally agreed markings relating to some hazards, and markings should as far as possible conform to such published standards as BS 5378[3] or as required by any appropriate legislation such as the Health and Safety (Safety Signs and Signals) Regulations 1996.[4,5]

Guidance 23

PUWER 98

ACOP 23

70 You should use a system of marking so that each power press, each guard, each protection device and each closed tool within the workplace is provided with a mark which will enable them to be uniquely identified.

PUWER 98

71 A letter or number systems of marking can be used. The simplest system is to provide each item with a unique number. But you can use a suitable supplier's identification mark instead.

72 Other possible systems include a reference to the type of equipment, for example 'Power Press A' , 'Fixed Guard 32', 'Closed Tool 23' or the use of the manufacturer's name followed by a letter or number. It is not necessary to include reference to the particular item within the mark, even where they have been given the same number, as long as the items cannot be confused with each other.

73 Whatever system of marking you use, the aim should be to make it flexible and as simple as possible. Marking systems which are cumbersome are less likely to be used successfully.

74 Remember that guarding systems may be transferred in whole or part between power presses and therefore it may not be appropriate to associate guards with particular presses through the identification mark.

75 A common error is for a system of guarding to be considered as a whole when in fact it is usually made up from several individual parts. For example, the fixed guarding around the tools of a power press in its simplest form may consist of at least four quite independent guards, ie front, back and sides. EACH guard needs to be treated as a separate item and marked appropriately.

76 Marking systems can be adapted or completely revised at any time. However, as the records of the thorough examination/test and of the inspection/test must be kept for at least two years and for six months respectively, you must be able to associate previous records with later ones.

77 Methods of marking the equipment include using indelible markers directly on the press frame and attaching small durable plates to guards. You should ensure that the marking is not easily damaged or easily removed.

Guidance 23

PUWER 98

Guidance 23

78 For closed tools the competent person may record the maximum permissible length of stroke of any press to be used with that tool and mark the information on it if considered necessary

PUWER 98

ACOP 23

79 You should mark each power press with the maximum permissible flywheel speed and the direction of rotation of the flywheel. Each mark should be clearly visible. The speed should be that specified by the press manufacturer.

PUWER 98

Guidance 23

80 The maximum permissible flywheel speed should be clearly marked to prevent overspeeding which can lead to overloading and failure of vital parts. The direction of rotation of the flywheel should be clearly marked as it should not be driven in the opposite direction to that marked, except in an emergency.

Regulation 31

Power presses to which Part IV does not apply

PUWER 98

Regulation 31

Regulations 32 to 35 shall not apply to a power press of a kind which is described in Schedule 2.

PUWER 98

Guidance 31

81 The regulations in Part IV of PUWER 98 cover thorough examination and inspection requirements. These regulations do not apply to the power presses listed in Schedule 2.

Regulation 32

Thorough examination of power presses, guards and protection devices

PUWER 98

(1) Every employer shall ensure that a power press is not put into service for the first time after installation, or after assembly at a new site or in a new location unless -

(a) it has been thoroughly examined to ensure that it -

(i) has been installed correctly; and

(ii) would be safe to operate; and

(b) any defect has been remedied.

(2) Every employer shall ensure that a guard, other than one to which paragraph (3) relates, or protection device is not put into service for the first time on a power press unless -

(a) it has been thoroughly examined when in position on that power press to ensure that it is effective for its purpose; and

(b) any defect has been remedied.

(3) Every employer shall ensure that that part of a closed tool which acts as a fixed guard is not used on a power press unless -

(a) it has been thoroughly examined when in position on any power press in the premises to ensure that it is effective for its purpose; and

(b) any defect has been remedied.

Regulation 31

PUWER 98

Guidance 32

82 The term 'competent person' (see paragraph 83) is not specifically referred to within regulation 32. It is within the definition of 'thorough examination' found under regulation 2(1).

PUWER 98

ACOP 32

Competent person

83 The person carrying out a thorough examination and test of a power press, guard, protection device or closed tool, should have sufficient practical and theoretical knowledge and experience to detect defects or weaknesses and assess their importance in relation to the safe operation and use of the power press.

PUWER 98

Guidance 32

84 Although it is not usual for competent persons to be employed by the organisation for whom the thorough examination is being carried out it is not prohibited by the Regulations. Where this is the case you should make arrangements to ensure that people carrying out the thorough examinations are not placed in situations where a conflict of interests could arise that would affect their professional judgement. They should remain independent from those directly involved in the day-to-day use of the power presses.

85 The Regulations do not stipulate the knowledge or qualifications for assessing the competency of people undertaking thorough examinations and testing. Such people will, however, need to possess such knowledge and experience of power press mechanisms and guards/protection devices to enable them to detect and assess the importance of defects which are, or may become, a cause of danger.

PUWER 98

ACOP 32

Thorough examination and test

86 A thorough examination and test of a power press should consist of such detailed examination, supplemented by removal of parts necessary to determine the safety of the press. The operations involved in carrying this out will depend on the type of press and on the judgement of the competent person. It should always include those parts concerned with the actuation or control of the slide and ram.

87 The thorough examination and test of a guard and/or protection device should consist of such careful visual examinations and dismantling as are necessary in order to verify its integrity. The thorough examination should always include any mechanism controlling a guard or protection device.

Testing

88 A suitable functional test should be carried out to confirm that a press, guard, and/or protection device is working properly and gives no indication of a fault.

PUWER 98

Guidance 32

89 A thorough examination carried out under regulation 32 always includes testing. This is provided for in the definition of 'thorough examination' under regulation 2(2).

90 Thorough examinations and tests of the power presses and the guards and/or protection devices should take place both after installation and at the specified intervals. However, there are special provisions for closed tools (see paragraphs 95 and 96).

PUWER 98

Guidance 32

Installation

91 The requirement for the thorough examination and testing of presses and their guards and/or protection devices, before they are first used in any workplace, is to ensure that they are properly installed and would be safe to operate. It also identifies old, worn, defective and obsolete presses and guards and/or protection devices, which frequently find their way into the second-hand market, and prevents their subsequent use unless and until these problems are corrected. It is intended also to prevent special-purpose presses being incorrectly used in conditions which might give rise to danger.

92 The Regulations do not contain an option for new guards and protection devices to receive their initial thorough examination on the press (whether old or new) for which they are intended at premises other than that where the press will be used. Although this was allowed under the Power Press Regulations the provision was rarely used.

93 If a guard or protection device for a tool is later moved to another press, then a further thorough examination and test must take place before it is used on that press. This must be carried out when it is in position on the press. However, subject to the requirements for periodical examinations, a guard or protection device does not need a thorough examination and test if it is moved to a press on which it has previously received a thorough examination and test, provided the report of the thorough examination and test is still valid and has not expired.

94 A guard or protection device which has been modified or altered should be treated as a new one.

Closed tool

95 Regulation 32(3) allows the initial thorough examination of the closed tool to be carried out on ANY press at the user's premises.

96 A further initial thorough examination and test is NOT required if the closed tool is later moved to a different power press. However, under regulation 33, if a closed tool is moved to another press or presses, it will still need to be inspected and tested before the press is used.

PUWER 98

Regulation 32

Periodic examination

(4) For the purpose of ensuring that health and safety conditions are maintained, and that any deterioration can be detected and remedied in good time, every employer shall ensure that -

(a) every power press is thoroughly examined, and its guards and protection devices are thoroughly examined when in position on that power press -

(i) at least every 12 months, where it has fixed guards only; or

(ii) at least every 6 months, in other cases; and

(iii) each time that exceptional circumstances have occurred which are liable to jeopardise the safety of the power press or its guards or protection devices; and

(b) any defect is remedied before the power press is used again.

Routine examination

97 After the initial thorough examinations and tests have been carried out, you should carry out the routine thorough examinations and tests of the press and its guards and/or protection devices. Regulation 32(4) specifies when these should be carried out.

98 Where the tools of a press are guarded entirely by fixed fencing, the press must not be used unless the press and the fixed guards have been thoroughly examined and tested by a competent person within the immediately preceding period of twelve months.

99 Where there is guarding other than fixed fencing (for example interlocked guarding or automatic guarding) which is used for all or part of the time, the press must not be used unless the press and the guards and/or protection devices have been thoroughly examined and tested by a competent person within the previous six months.

Exceptional circumstances

100 Exceptional circumstances (see regulation 32(4)(a)(iii)) which may result in the need for a thorough examination include:

(a) major modifications, refurbishment or major repair work;

(b) known or suspected serious damage;

(c) substantial change in the nature of use.

101 A thorough examination would be necessary under these circumstances whether the six- or twelve-month thorough examination is due or not.

Thorough examination

102 The regulation does not specify the operations that are involved in the thorough examination and test of a power press and the guards and/or protection devices. What is required is a thorough examination and test of a power press and the guards and/or protection device which will enable the competent person to make a true report, containing the particulars in Schedule 3, of the condition of the press and the guards and/or protection devices.

103 The condition of the parts of the press which actuate and control the slide or ram are crucial to its safe operation, which is why they need to be included in the thorough examination.

Positive clutch press

104 For positive clutch presses, the competent person needs to be satisfied of the condition of items such as the key, the key spring, the flywheel journal and flywheel bearing bush. To verify that these items are in a serviceable condition, and to enable them to be checked for potentially dangerous defects such as hair cracks in keys and chipped keyways, it will sometimes be essential to fully or partly remove the flywheel. When second-hand presses are thoroughly examined after installation the flywheel should always be fully or partly removed.

Guidance 32

PUWER 98

Friction clutch presses

105 At friction clutch presses where the flywheel runs in plain bearings, similar criteria to those in paragraph 104 should usually be applied. At friction clutch presses where the flywheel runs in ball or roller bearings, including needle bearings, complete or partial withdrawal should not normally be necessary but the competent person may find evidence that it would be advisable.

Other types of press

106 Certain types of geared presses have a flywheel which rotates on ball and roller bearings resting on a quill anchored to the main frame. The main drive shaft passes through this quill. If the flywheel bearings were to fail, the flywheel would be brought to a standstill and it would not be possible to transmit the drive to the crank (or eccentric) shaft. In these circumstances there would be no point in removing or partly withdrawing the flywheel.

Guard or protection device

107 There is a requirement for the periodic thorough examination and test by the competent person of fixed guards at six- or twelve-month intervals. This means that at every thorough examination and test the competent person will need to establish that the entire guarding system is effective.

108 The thorough examination of a guard and/or protection device should verify its integrity. This must always take place when it is actually in position on the installed power press on which it is to be used.

Testing

109 The tests of power presses and guards and/or protection devices are intended to supplement the thorough examination. In most cases all that is needed is a functional test. The competent person needs to confirm that the press and guard/protection device is working properly and gives no indication of any fault not disclosed by the thorough examination.

110 Where an arrestor brake is used together with a guard which opens at the end of a downstroke and the brake is relied upon to prevent overrun past top dead centre, the thorough examination should include a test of the brake. The test should be carried out according to the manufacturer's instructions.

Guidance 32

PUWER 98

Transitional periods

(5) Where a power press, guard or protection device was before the coming into force of these Regulations required to be thoroughly examined by regulation 5(2) or the Power Presses Regulations 1965[(a)] the first thorough examination under paragraph (4) shall be made before the date by which a thorough examination would have been required by regulation 5(2) had it remained in force.

(a) SI 1965/1441.

Regulation 32

PUWER 98

111 Regulation 32(5) allows a transition period for change over of thorough examinations required under regulation 5(2) of the Power Presses Regulations 1965 and regulation 32(4) of PUWER 98.

112 If you have had a thorough examination carried out under the Power Presses Regulations 1965 you do not have to have the power press, guard or protection device examined again until before it would have been required under those Regulations although they have been replaced by PUWER 98.

Guidance 32

PUWER 98

Regulation 32

Closed tools

(6) Paragraph (4) shall not apply to that part of a closed tool which acts as a fixed guard.

PUWER 98

Guidance 32

113 Closed tools do not need to be thoroughly examined and tested under regulation 32(4) because they are excluded by regulation 32(6). Closed tools still require a daily inspection and test by the setter (regulation 33(1)).

PUWER 98

Regulation 32

Defect

(7) In this regulation "defect" means a defect notified under regulation 34 other than a defect which has not yet become a danger to persons.

PUWER 98

Guidance 32

114 The word 'defect' is used frequently throughout PUWER 98 in relation to the press and guard and/or protection device. Where it is used within this regulation, it is referring to:

(a) a safety problem with the equipment which is serious enough to warrant that it should not be used; or

(b) a safety problem for which there is a period specified in the report of thorough examination and test for suitable remedial action.

115 In case (a), if the competent person notifies you of any defect disclosed in a power press or the guard and/or protection device as a result of the thorough examination and test then the press or guards/protection devices may not be used until the defect is remedied.

116 In case (b), if the competent person specifies in their notification to you a period within which the defect ought to be remedied and that period has passed, then the press or guard/protection device may not be used unless the defect has been remedied.

Remedial action

117 As soon as any notified defect has been remedied, you should make a record of the remedial action taken and the date when this was done. This information can be entered on the report of the related thorough examination and test or as a separate report.

Regulation 33 Inspection of guards and protection devices

PUWER 98

Regulation 33

(1) Every employer shall ensure that a power press is not used after the setting, re-setting or adjustment of its tools, save in trying out its tools or save in die proving, unless -

(a) its every guard and protection device has been inspected and tested while in position on the power press by a person appointed in writing by the employer who is -

(i) competent; or

(ii) undergoing training for that purpose and acting under the immediate supervision of a competent person,

and who has signed a certificate which complies with paragraph (3); or

PUWER 98

Regulation 33

> (b) *the guards and protection devices have not been altered or disturbed in the course of the adjustment of its tools.*

(2) Every employer shall ensure that a power press is not used after the expiration of the fourth hour of a working period unless its every guard and protection device has been inspected and tested while in position on the power press by a person appointed in writing by the employer who is -

> (a) *competent; or*
>
> (b) *undergoing training for that purpose and acting under the immediate supervision of a competent person,*

and who has signed a certificate which complies with paragraph (3).

PUWER 98

ACOP 33

Appointed person

118 You should ensure that the person you appoint for the purpose of this regulation has received suitable and sufficient training, before being allowed to inspect and test a guard and/or protection device on their own. An appointed person who is undergoing training may carry out inspections, providing they are acting under the immediate supervision of a person already appointed. In addition they should have the competence, maturity and authority appropriate to the circumstances.

PUWER 98

Guidance 33

119 Before a person can be allowed to carry out inspection and testing on their own, you must ensure that for each class or description of power press, guard and protection device on which they will work that they:

(a) have been adequately trained;

(b) are competent to carry out the duties; and

(c) have been appointed in writing.

120 People undergoing training for inspection and testing are also required to be appointed and must always work under the immediate supervision of an appointed person, who is competent, until they have completed their training. The level of supervision should be appropriate to the stage in the training they have reached, competency demonstrated, and also to the particular job being carried out.

121 You may record these appointments by means of signed and dated entries in a register or by signed and dated certificates attached to it. The appointment should make it clear if the appointed persons are undergoing training and it should then specify which people are required to provide immediate supervision of the work.

122 The register or certificate can specify each class or description of power press, guard and protection device for which the person is appointed. If the appointment is revoked, this can also be recorded. You can give copies of the entry or certificate of appointment to the person concerned.

123 An ACOP and guidance on training can be found in paragraphs 61-66.

Authority and maturity

124 In addition to being technically competent to carry out inspection and testing of guards and protection devices, people should also have the

PUWER 98

appropriate maturity and authority for the circumstances. Pressures can arise where production needs conflict with the requirement to carry out the 'daily' inspection and test within the first four hours. Circumstances have also occurred where the person carrying out the inspection identifies that the press is dangerous to use and must prevent any further use of the press. When such situations arise, it is vital that the individual can be relied on to provide timely and objective reports of their inspection and test. This is less likely to be a problem for an employee with both authority and maturity.

125 The inspection and test is required to identify day-to-day deterioration of guards and protection devices and to ensure their integrity following setting, resetting or adjustment of tools. If the person appointed does not carry out their job correctly, press operators could be seriously injured. People with suitable maturity are more likely to accept this responsibility and act accordingly.

Guidance 33

PUWER 98

Inspection

126 You should ensure that an inspection, by the appointed person, of a guard or protection device under regulation 33, consists of appropriate visual inspection of those parts that can be seen. This should include a suitable test to assess the correct functioning and integrity of the guard and/or protection device, including that part of a closed tool which acts as a guard, in use.

ACOP 33

PUWER 98

127 This regulation requires an inspection and test of guards and/or protection devices in two circumstances. These are set out in paragraphs 128-129. All inspections and tests should be directed at discovering defects in guards and/or protection devices; at checking that they are suitable for the press and the tools that are fitted to it, that they are properly in position on the presses; and at ensuring that they are in effective working order. The test which is required is a simple functional one to verify that the guards and/or protection devices are working properly.

Action after setting, re-setting or adjustment of tools

128 A POWER PRESS MUST NOT BE USED AFTER THE TOOLS ON THE PRESS HAVE BEEN SET, RE-SET OR ADJUSTED UNLESS EVERY GUARD AND/OR INSPECTION DEVICE ON THE PRESS HAS BEEN INSPECTED AND TESTED BY AN APPOINTED PERSON AND THEY HAVE SIGNED THE DAILY LOG TO SHOW THIS. However, where the work at the press tools is no more than adjustment and the adjustment has not resulted in any alteration to or disturbance of any guard or protection device on the press, then no new inspection and test is required provided that the appointed person verifies that the guards and/ or protection devices remain effective. (Note: Under regulation 11 of PUWER 98, the tools must be guarded, whenever they constitute a dangerous part of machinery, when a trial stroke is made.)

Action before or during the first four hours of each working period

129 A power press must not be used after the first four hours of any working period have passed, unless it has been inspected and tested and a certificate given:

(a) at any time before the start of the working period and after the press was last used; or

(b) at any time within the first four hours of the working period.

130 Where the fourth hour has passed, an inspection and test must be carried

Guidance 33

PUWER 98

out if you wish to use the press during the latter part of the working period. In this case, however, the inspection and test must take place before the press is used.

131 The purpose of this requirement is to ensure that guards and protection devices are inspected and tested, by a suitably qualified person, daily while they are in use or, if you are operating a shift system, once during every shift when they are in use.

132 This inspection/test is best carried out before the day's work (or the shift) begins. However, this is not always possible, for example because of continuous shift work or because a large number of presses are being used. This is the reason why the inspection and testing can take place up to four hours after the start of the working period.

133 Where an inspection and test immediately follows tool setting, re-setting or adjustment and has been carried out within the period referred to in paragraph 129, no further inspection or test will be required in that working period unless the tools are again set, re-set or adjusted. For example, in a workplace with working hours only from 8 am to 4 pm, any inspection and test (following tool setting, re-setting or adjustment) which is carried out between 12 noon and 4 pm would not enable an employer to dispense with the inspection and test required under regulation 33(2) for that day. On the other hand, an inspection and test immediately after tools have been set, re-set or adjusted which has been carried out after work has ceased on one day and not later than 12 noon on the next day, would also meet the requirement for an inspection and test under regulation 33(2) on that next day.

Guidance 33

PUWER 98

(3) A certificate referred to in this regulation shall -

(a) contain sufficient particulars to identify every guard and protection device inspected and tested and the power press on which it was positioned at the time of the inspection and test;

(b) state the date and time of the inspection and test; and

(c) state that every guard and protection device on the power press is in position and effective for its purpose.

Regulation 33

PUWER 98
ACOP 33

134 The certificate may be a card that is signed or initialled for every inspection.

PUWER 98

135 The certificate is, in effect, a certificate of fitness for use. The person making the inspection and test should ignore any defect already notified to you as a result of a thorough examination and test if the period specified for correction has not expired and the defect has not become a cause of danger.

Guidance 33

PUWER 98

(4) In this regulation "working period", in relation to a power press, means -

(a) the period in which the day's or night's work is done; or

(b) in premises where a shift system is in operation, a shift.

Regulation 33

Regulation 34

Reports

PUWER 98

(1) A person making a thorough examination for an employer under regulation 32 shall -

(a) notify the employer forthwith of any defect in a power press or its guard or protection device which in his opinion is or could become a danger to persons;

(b) as soon as is practicable make a report of the thorough examination to the employer in writing authenticated by him or on his behalf by signature or equally secure means and containing the information specified in Schedule 3; and

(c) where there is in his opinion a defect in a power press or its guard or protection device which is or could become a danger to persons, send a copy of the report as soon as is practicable to the enforcing authority for the premises in which the power press is situated.

Regulation 34

PUWER 98

Notification of defects

136 For the purposes of regulation 34(1)(a), 'forthwith' means that where a competent person finds a defect in a power press or guard or protection device which in his opinion is, or could become, a risk to safety, before the competent person leaves the work place they should inform the employer or their representative of this.

ACOP 34

PUWER 98

137 Immediate notification of defects is normally given separately. However, a report containing the information specified in Schedule 3 for the thorough examination and test for notifying defects to the user can be used providing it does not delay the requirement to notify 'forthwith'.

Guidance 34

PUWER 98

Thorough examination reports

138 A report should be made of every thorough examination and be submitted no later than 14 days after the examination. Any suitable method of reporting may be used subject to agreement between the employer and the competent person.

ACOP 34

PUWER 98

139 A signature for the purposes of regulation 34(1)(b) means the report should be authenticated in some way.

140 A report of any thorough examination and test should be made by the competent person who has carried it out. It should contain the information specified in Schedule 3.

Reporting to the enforcing authority

141 Where a defect (or defects) has been reported to the user a copy of the report containing the information specified in Schedule 3 must also be sent to the enforcing authority by the competent person.

Guidance 34

PUWER 98

(2) A person making an inspection and test for an employer under regulation 33 shall forthwith notify the employer of any defect in a guard or protection device which in his opinion is or could become a danger to persons and the reason for his opinion.

Regulation 34

PUWER 98

ACOP 34

Inspection reports

142 When an appointed person carries out an inspection under regulation 33 and finds a defect, he should tell the employer or his representative immediately, and should not sign the certificate. Defects would include a missing guard or protection device that is not in position, not properly in position or in their opinion, is not suitable.

Regulation 35

Keeping of information

PUWER 98

Regulation 35

(1) Every employer shall ensure that the information in every report made pursuant to regulation 34(1) is kept available for inspection for 2 years after it is made.

(2) Every employer shall ensure that a certificate under regulation 33(1)(a)(ii) or (2)(b) is kept available for inspection -

(a) at or near the power press to which it relates until superseded by a later certificate; and

(b) after that, until 6 months have passed since it was signed.

PUWER 98

Guidance 35

143 The reports and certificates must be kept available for any inspector of health and safety to see for two years and for six months respectively.

144 While a certificate of an inspection and test is current it should be kept on or near the power press to which it relates. You will often find it convenient to provide a holder on the press for this purpose. After expiry, all certificates must be kept available for inspection for a period of six months.

Regulation 38

Repeal of enactment

PUWER 98

Regulation 38

Section 19 of the Offices, Shops and Railway Premises Act 1963 is repealed[(a)].

(a) 1963 c.41

Regulation 39

Revocation of instruments

PUWER 98

Regulation 39

The instruments specified in column 1 of Schedule 4 are revoked to the extent specified in column 3 of that Schedule.

Schedule 2

Power presses to which regulations 32 to 35 do not apply

Schedule

2

Regulation 31

1 *A power press for the working of hot metal.*

2 *A power press not capable of a stroke greater than six mm.*

3 *A guillotine.*

4 *A combination punching and shearing machine, turret punch press or similar machine for punching, shearing or cropping.*

5 *A machine, other than a press brake, for bending steel sections.*

6 *A straightening machine.*

7 *An upsetting machine.*

8 *A heading machine.*

9 *A riveting machine.*

10 *An eyeletting machine.*

11 *A press-stud attaching machine.*

12 *A zip fastener bottom stop attaching machine.*

13 *A stapling machine.*

14 *A wire stitching machine.*

15 *A power press for the compacting of metal powders.*

Schedule 3

Information to be contained in a report of a thorough examination of a power press, guard or protection device

Schedule 3

Regulation 34(1)(b)

1 *The name of the employer for whom the thorough examination was made.*

2 *The address of the premises at which the thorough examination was made.*

3 *In relation to each item examined -*

(a) *that it is a power press, interlocking guard, fixed guard or other type of guard or protection device;*

(b) *where known its make, type and year of manufacture;*

(c) *the identifying mark of -*

(i) *the manufacturer;*

(ii) *the employer.*

4 *In relation to the first thorough examination of a power press after installation or after assembly at a new site or in a new location -*

(a) *that it is such thorough examination;*

(b) *either that it has been installed correctly and would be safe to operate or the respects in which it has not been installed correctly or would not be safe to operate;*

(c) *identification of any part found to have a defect, and a description of the defect.*

5 *In relation to a thorough examination of a power press other than one to which paragraph 4 relates -*

(a) *that it is such other thorough examination;*

(b) *either that the power press would be safe to operate or the respects in which it would not be safe to operate;*

(c) *identification of any part found to have a defect which is or could become a danger to persons, and a description of the defect.*

6 *In relation to a thorough examination of a guard or protection device -*

(a) *either that it is effective for its purpose or the respects in which it is not effective for its purpose;*

(b) *identification of any part found to have a defect which is or could become a danger to persons, and a description of the defect.*

7 *Any repair, renewal or alteration required to remedy a defect found to be a danger to persons.*

8 *In the case of a defect which is not yet but could become a danger to persons -*

(a) the time by which it could become such danger;

(b) any repair, renewal or alteration required to remedy it.

9 *Any other defect which requires remedy.*

10 *Any repair, renewal or alteration referred to in paragraph 7 which has already been effected.*

11 *The date on which any defect referred to in paragraph 8 was notified to the employer under regulation 34(1)(a).*

12 *The qualification and address of the person making the report; that he is self-employed or, if employed, the name and address of his employer.*

13 *The date of the thorough examination.*

14 *The date of the report.*

15 *The name of the person making the report and where different the name of the person signing or otherwise authenticating it.*

Schedule 4

Revocation of instruments

Schedule

Regulation 39

(1) *Title*	*(2)* *Reference*	*(3)* *Extent of revocation*
The Operations at Unfenced Machinery (Amended Schedule) Regulations 1946	S.R. & O. 1946/156	The whole Regulations
The Agriculture (Circular Saws) Regulations 1959	S.I. 1959/427	The whole Regulations
The Prescribed Dangerous Machines Order 1964	S.I. 1964/971	The whole Order
The Power Presses Regulations 1965	S.I. 1965/1441	The whole Regulations
The Abrasive Wheels Regulations 1970	S.I. 1970/535	The whole Regulations
The Power Presses (Amendment) Regulations 1972	S.I. 1972/1512	The whole Regulations
The Woodworking Machines Regulation 1974	S.I. 1974/903	The whole Regulations
The Operations at Unfenced Machinery (Amendment) Regulations 1976	S.I. 1976/955	The whole Regulations
The Factories (Standards of Lighting) (Revocation) Regulations 1978	S.I. 1978/1126	The whole Regulations
The Offshore Installations (Application of Statutory Instruments) Regulations 1984	S.I. 1984/419	The whole Regulations
The Offshore Installations (Operational Safety, Health and Welfare and Life-Saving Appliances) (Revocations) Regulations 1989	S.I. 1989/1672	The whole Regulations
The Provision and Use of Work Equipment Regulations 1992	S.I. 1992/2932	The whole Regulations
The Construction (Health, Safety and Welfare) Regulations 1996	S.I. 1996/1592	Regulation 27

4

References

1 *Safe use of work equipment. The Provision and Use of Work Equipment Regulations 1998. Approved Code of Practice and Guidance on Regulations* L22 HSE Books ISBN 0 7176 1626 6

2 *Consulting employees on health and safety at law: a guide to the law* INDG232 HSE Books (single copies free; ISBN 0 7176 1615 0 for priced packs of 15 copies)

3 BS 5378 *Safety signs and colours* - Part 1 *Colour and design* (1980); Part 2 *Colormetric and photometric properties of material* (1980); Part 3 *Specification for additional signs to those given in BS 5378: Part 1* (1982)

4 *Safety signs and signals. The Health and Safety (Safety Signs and Signals) Regulations 1996. Guidance on Regulations* L64 HSE Books ISBN 0 7176 0870 0

5 *Signpost to the Health and Safety (Safety Signs and Signals) Regulations 1996* INDG184 HSE Books (single copies free; ISBN 0 7176 1139 6 for priced packs of 15 copies)

Printed and published by the Health and Safety Executive 12/98 C200